ANNE GEDDES

Copyright © 2000 Anne Geddes
www.annegeddes.com
The right of Anne Geddes to be identified as the Author
of the Work has been asserted by her in accordance with the
Copyright, Designs and Patents Act 1988.

First published in 2000 by Photogenique Publishers
(a division of Hodder Moa Beckett)
Studio 3.16, Axis Building, 1 Cleveland Road, Parnell
Auckland, New Zealand

Published in Great Britain in 2000
by HEADLINE BOOK PUBLISHING
A division of the Hodder Headline Group
338 Euston Road, London NW1 3BH

10 9 8 7 6 5 4 3 2 1

Produced by Kel Geddes
Colour separations by MH Group

Printed by Midas Printing Limited, Hong Kong

All rights reserved. No part of this publication may be reproduced, stored in
a retrieval system, or transmitted, in any form or by any means without the prior written
permission of the publisher, nor be otherwise circulated in any form of binding or cover
other than that in which it is published and without a similar condition being imposed
on the subsequent purchaser.

British Library Cataloguing in Publication Data
for this title is available on request.

ISBN 0 7472 7269 7

*The publishers are grateful for the permission to reproduce those items
which are subject to copyright. While every effort has been made
to trace copyright holders, the publishers would be pleased to hear from
any they were unable to contact.*

ANNE GEDDES
Thoughts with Love

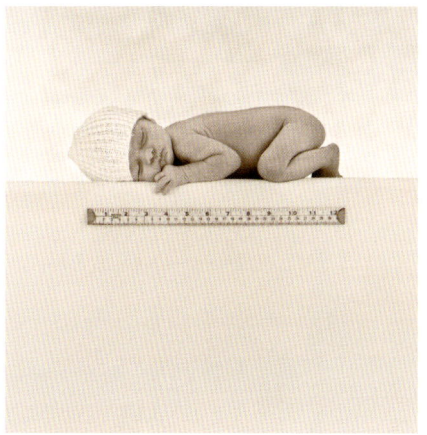

Birthdays & Anniversaries

January Birthdays

Name

Birth date

Star sign

Gift ideas

Name

Birth date

Star sign

Gift ideas

Name

Birth date

Star sign

Gift ideas

Name

Birth date

Star sign

Gift ideas

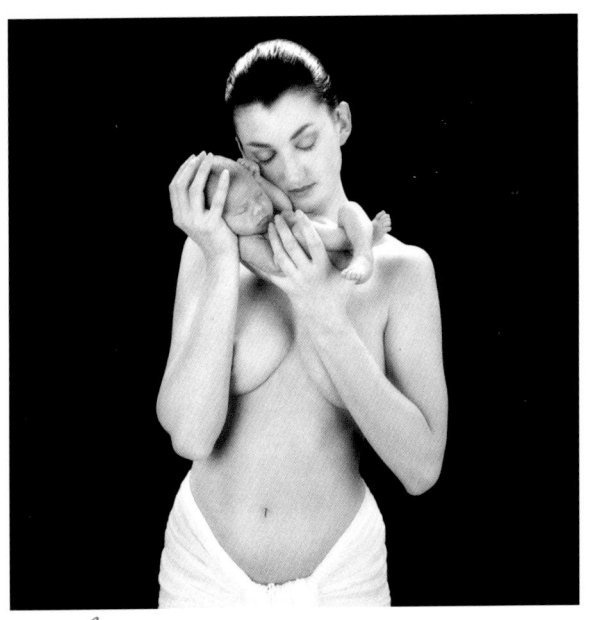

A mother understands what a child does not say.

Proverb

January Birthdays

Name

Birth date

Star sign

Gift ideas

Name

Birth date

Star sign

Gift ideas

Name

Birth date

Star sign

Gift ideas

Name

Birth date

Star sign

Gift ideas

*S*mall is beautiful.

Proverb

January Birthdays

Name

Birth date

Star sign

Gift ideas

Name

Birth date

Star sign

Gift ideas

Name

Birth date

Star sign

Gift ideas

Name

Birth date

Star sign

Gift ideas

January Anniversaries

Name

Date

Occasion

Gift ideas

Name

Date

Occasion

Gift ideas

Name

Date

Occasion

Gift ideas

Name

Date

Occasion

Gift ideas

February Birthdays

Name

Birth date

Star sign

Gift ideas

Name

Birth date

Star sign

Gift ideas

Name

Birth date

Star sign

Gift ideas

Name

Birth date

Star sign

Gift ideas

The decision to have a child is to accept that your heart will forever walk about outside of your body.

Katharine Hadley

February Birthdays

Name

Birth date

Star sign

Gift ideas

Name

Birth date

Star sign

Gift ideas

Name

Birth date

Star sign

Gift ideas

Name

Birth date

Star sign

Gift ideas

Babies are such a nice way to start people.

Don Herold (1889–1966)

February Birthdays

Name

Birth date

Star sign

Gift ideas

Name

Birth date

Star sign

Gift ideas

Name

Birth date

Star sign

Gift ideas

Name

Birth date

Star sign

Gift ideas

February Anniversaries

Name

Date

Occasion

Gift ideas

Name

Date

Occasion

Gift ideas

Name

Date

Occasion

Gift ideas

Name

Date

Occasion

Gift ideas

March Birthdays

Name

Birth date

Star sign

Gift ideas

Name

Birth date

Star sign

Gift ideas

Name

Birth date

Star sign

Gift ideas

Name

Birth date

Star sign

Gift ideas

From small beginnings come great things.

Proverb

March Birthdays

Name

Birth date

Star sign

Gift ideas

Name

Birth date

Star sign

Gift ideas

Name

Birth date

Star sign

Gift ideas

Name

Birth date

Star sign

Gift ideas

𝒯ears ... the diamonds of the eye.

Rev. Dr. Davies

March Birthdays

Name

Birth date

Star sign

Gift ideas

Name

Birth date

Star sign

Gift ideas

Name

Birth date

Star sign

Gift ideas

Name

Birth date

Star sign

Gift ideas

March Anniversaries

Name

Date

Occasion

Gift ideas

Name

Date

Occasion

Gift ideas

Name

Date

Occasion

Gift ideas

Name

Date

Occasion

Gift ideas

April Birthdays

Name

Birth date

Star sign

Gift ideas

Name

Birth date

Star sign

Gift ideas

Name

Birth date

Star sign

Gift ideas

Name

Birth date

Star sign

Gift ideas

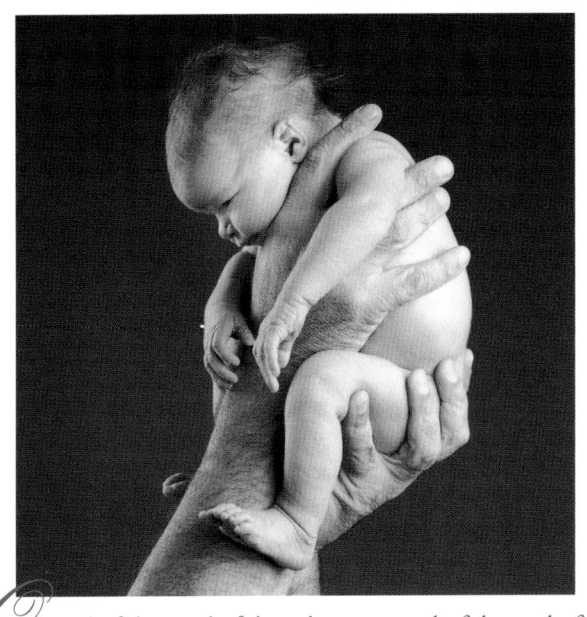

O wonderful, wonderful, and most wonderful wonderful!
and yet again wonderful.

William Shakespeare (1564–1616)

April Birthdays

Name

Birth date

Star sign

Gift ideas

Name

Birth date

Star sign

Gift ideas

Name

Birth date

Star sign

Gift ideas

Name

Birth date

Star sign

Gift ideas

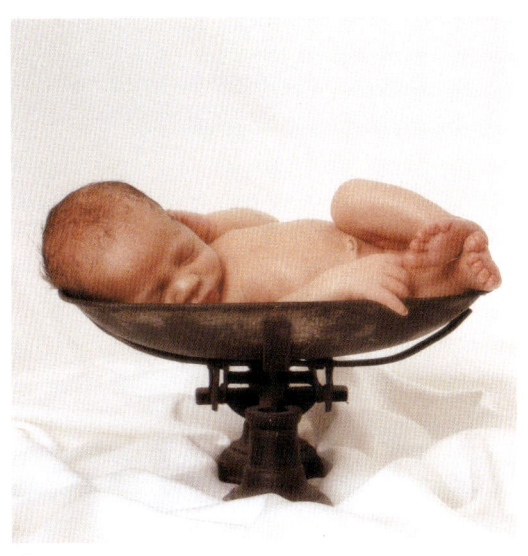

𝒜 perfect example of minority rule is a baby in the house.

Anonymous

April Birthdays

Name

Birth date

Star sign

Gift ideas

Name

Birth date

Star sign

Gift ideas

Name

Birth date

Star sign

Gift ideas

Name

Birth date

Star sign

Gift ideas

April Anniversaries

Name

Date

Occasion

Gift ideas

Name

Date

Occasion

Gift ideas

Name

Date

Occasion

Gift ideas

Name

Date

Occasion

Gift ideas

May Birthdays

Name

Birth date

Star sign

Gift ideas

Name

Birth date

Star sign

Gift ideas

Name

Birth date

Star sign

Gift ideas

Name

Birth date

Star sign

Gift ideas

Do you believe in fairies?
... If you believe, clap your hands!

J. M. Barrie (1860–1937)

May Birthdays

Name

Birth date

Star sign

Gift ideas

Name

Birth date

Star sign

Gift ideas

Name

Birth date

Star sign

Gift ideas

Name

Birth date

Star sign

Gift ideas

A new baby is like the beginning of all things – wonder, hope, a dream of possibilities.

Eda J. Leshan (1922–)

May Birthdays

Name

Birth date

Star sign

Gift ideas

Name

Birth date

Star sign

Gift ideas

Name

Birth date

Star sign

Gift ideas

Name

Birth date

Star sign

Gift ideas

May Anniversaries

Name

Date

Occasion

Gift ideas

Name

Date

Occasion

Gift ideas

Name

Date

Occasion

Gift ideas

Name

Date

Occasion

Gift ideas

June Birthdays

Name

Birth date

Star sign

Gift ideas

Name

Birth date

Star sign

Gift ideas

Name

Birth date

Star sign

Gift ideas

Name

Birth date

Star sign

Gift ideas

*L*ittle children are the most lovely flowers this side of Eden.

Rev. Dr. Davies

June Birthdays

Name

Birth date

Star sign

Gift ideas

Name

Birth date

Star sign

Gift ideas

Name

Birth date

Star sign

Gift ideas

Name

Birth date

Star sign

Gift ideas

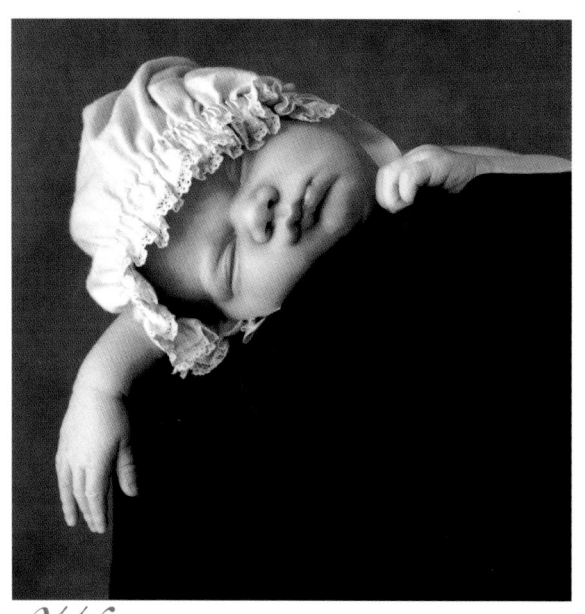

*W*hisper in your sleeping child's ear, "I love you."

H. Jackson Brown, Jr. (1940–)

June Birthdays

Name

Birth date

Star sign

Gift ideas

Name

Birth date

Star sign

Gift ideas

Name

Birth date

Star sign

Gift ideas

Name

Birth date

Star sign

Gift ideas

June Anniversaries

Name

Date

Occasion

Gift ideas

Name

Date

Occasion

Gift ideas

Name

Date

Occasion

Gift ideas

Name

Date

Occasion

Gift ideas

July Birthdays

Name

Birth date

Star sign

Gift ideas

Name

Birth date

Star sign

Gift ideas

Name

Birth date

Star sign

Gift ideas

Name

Birth date

Star sign

Gift ideas

*L*ife itself is the most wonderful fairy tale.

Hans Christian Andersen (1805–1875)

July Birthdays

Name

Birth date

Star sign

Gift ideas

Name

Birth date

Star sign

Gift ideas

Name

Birth date

Star sign

Gift ideas

Name

Birth date

Star sign

Gift ideas

How soft and fresh he breathes!
Look! He is dreaming! Visions sure of joy
Are gladdening his rest; and, ah! who knows
But waiting angels do converse in sleep
With babes like this!

Bishop Coxe (1818–1896)

July Birthdays

Name

Birth date

Star sign

Gift ideas

Name

Birth date

Star sign

Gift ideas

Name

Birth date

Star sign

Gift ideas

Name

Birth date

Star sign

Gift ideas

July Anniversaries

Name

Date

Occasion

Gift ideas

Name

Date

Occasion

Gift ideas

Name

Date

Occasion

Gift ideas

Name

Date

Occasion

Gift ideas

August Birthdays

Name

Birth date

Star sign

Gift ideas

Name

Birth date

Star sign

Gift ideas

Name

Birth date

Star sign

Gift ideas

Name

Birth date

Star sign

Gift ideas

*I*t was the Rainbow gave thee birth,
And left thee all her lovely hues.

William Henry Davies (1871–1940)

August Birthdays

Name

Birth date

Star sign

Gift ideas

Name

Birth date

Star sign

Gift ideas

Name

Birth date

Star sign

Gift ideas

Name

Birth date

Star sign

Gift ideas

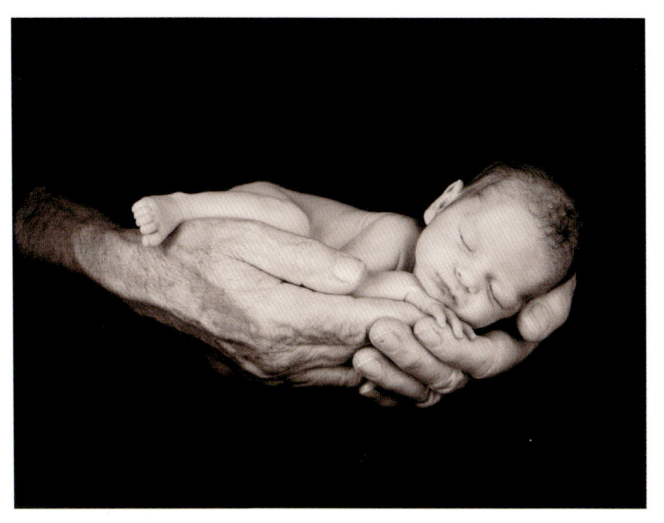

We can do no great things – only small things with great love.

Mother Teresa (1910–1997)

August Birthdays

Name

Birth date

Star sign

Gift ideas

Name

Birth date

Star sign

Gift ideas

Name

Birth date

Star sign

Gift ideas

Name

Birth date

Star sign

Gift ideas

August Anniversaries

Name

Date

Occasion

Gift ideas

Name

Date

Occasion

Gift ideas

Name

Date

Occasion

Gift ideas

Name

Date

Occasion

Gift ideas

September Birthdays

Name

Birth date

Star sign

Gift ideas

Name

Birth date

Star sign

Gift ideas

Name

Birth date

Star sign

Gift ideas

Name

Birth date

Star sign

Gift ideas

The very pink of perfection.

Oliver Goldsmith (1728–1774)

September Birthdays

Name

Birth date

Star sign

Gift ideas

Name

Birth date

Star sign

Gift ideas

Name

Birth date

Star sign

Gift ideas

Name

Birth date

Star sign

Gift ideas

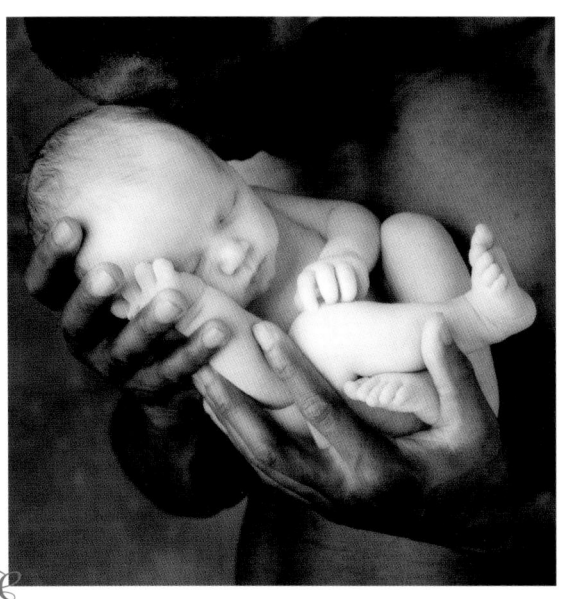

$\mathscr{E}$ach day I love you more ... today, more than yesterday ...
and less than tomorrow.

Rosemonde Gérard

September Birthdays

Name

Birth date

Star sign

Gift ideas

Name

Birth date

Star sign

Gift ideas

Name

Birth date

Star sign

Gift ideas

Name

Birth date

Star sign

Gift ideas

September Anniversaries

Name

Date

Occasion

Gift ideas

Name

Date

Occasion

Gift ideas

Name

Date

Occasion

Gift ideas

Name

Date

Occasion

Gift ideas

October Birthdays

Name

Birth date

Star sign

Gift ideas

Name

Birth date

Star sign

Gift ideas

Name

Birth date

Star sign

Gift ideas

Name

Birth date

Star sign

Gift ideas

You should have a softer pillow than my heart.

Lord Byron (1788–1824)

October Birthdays

Name

Birth date

Star sign

Gift ideas

Name

Birth date

Star sign

Gift ideas

Name

Birth date

Star sign

Gift ideas

Name

Birth date

Star sign

Gift ideas

Happiness is the intoxication produced by the moment of poise between a satisfactory past, and an immediate future, rich with promise.

Ella Maillart (1903–)

October Birthdays

Name

Birth date

Star sign

Gift ideas

Name

Birth date

Star sign

Gift ideas

Name

Birth date

Star sign

Gift ideas

Name

Birth date

Star sign

Gift ideas

October Anniversaries

Name

Date

Occasion

Gift ideas

Name

Date

Occasion

Gift ideas

Name

Date

Occasion

Gift ideas

Name

Date

Occasion

Gift ideas

November Birthdays

Name

Birth date

Star sign

Gift ideas

Name

Birth date

Star sign

Gift ideas

Name

Birth date

Star sign

Gift ideas

Name

Birth date

Star sign

Gift ideas

*Kiss your children goodnight,
even if they are already asleep.*

H. Jackson Brown, Jr. (1940–)

November Birthdays

Name

Birth date

Star sign

Gift ideas

Name

Birth date

Star sign

Gift ideas

Name

Birth date

Star sign

Gift ideas

Name

Birth date

Star sign

Gift ideas

The smiles of infants are said to be
the first fruits of human reason.

Rev. Henry N. Hudson

November Birthdays

Name

Birth date

Star sign

Gift ideas

Name

Birth date

Star sign

Gift ideas

Name

Birth date

Star sign

Gift ideas

Name

Birth date

Star sign

Gift ideas

November Anniversaries

Name

Date

Occasion

Gift ideas

Name

Date

Occasion

Gift ideas

Name

Date

Occasion

Gift ideas

Name

Date

Occasion

Gift ideas

December Birthdays

Name

Birth date

Star sign

Gift ideas

Name

Birth date

Star sign

Gift ideas

Name

Birth date

Star sign

Gift ideas

Name

Birth date

Star sign

Gift ideas

I have spread my dreams under your feet;
Tread softly because you tread on my dreams.

W. B. Yeats (1865–1939)

December Birthdays

Name

Birth date

Star sign

Gift ideas

Name

Birth date

Star sign

Gift ideas

Name

Birth date

Star sign

Gift ideas

Name

Birth date

Star sign

Gift ideas

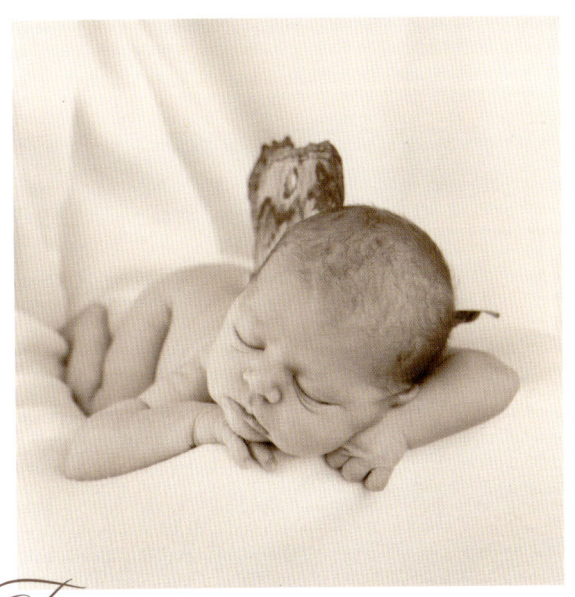

There are only two lasting bequests we can hope to give our children. One of these is roots; the other, wings.

Cecilia Lasbury

December Birthdays

Name

Birth date

Star sign

Gift ideas

Name

Birth date

Star sign

Gift ideas

Name

Birth date

Star sign

Gift ideas

Name

Birth date

Star sign

Gift ideas

December Anniversaries

Name

Date

Occasion

Gift ideas

Name

Date

Occasion

Gift ideas

Name

Date

Occasion

Gift ideas

Name

Date

Occasion

Gift ideas

STAR SIGNS

ANNIVERSARIES

BIRTHSTONES & FLOWERS

STAR SIGNS

AQUARIUS *20 January – 18 February*

Eccentric, uncompromising, unconventional and unpredictable, Aquarians hate pretence. They are great intellectual snobs, but they're definitely not social ones and instead are often committed humanitarians with strong social and political consciences. In fact their love for humans in general often overrides their love of individuals – they are hard to get to know intimately and find difficulty forming long-term relationships. They love to argue, and will come up with innovative ideas, but they fall short in applying them. They are natural performers. In their desire for freedom, they tend to shun the constraints of conventional marriages.

Perfect partner: Scorpio.

Disasters: Cancer.

PISCES *19 February – 20 March*

The original chameleons, elusive Pisceans constantly change their feelings and ideas and will see something of value in everything – even opposites. They are very intuitive, sensitive and idealistic, but often lack common sense. They hate confrontations, and have the knack of seeming compliant while continuing to do exactly as they please. They can become visionaries or mystics, but at their worst may embrace the escapism offered by drugs or alcohol. They are great romantics, known for their desire to see everything through rose-coloured glasses, but in their search for an ideal soul mate they are frequently drawn to domineering types.

Perfect partners: Capricorn, Taurus.

Disasters: Gemini.

STAR SIGNS

ARIES *21 March – 19 April*

Optimistic, assertive and lively, Arians throw themselves headlong at life. They know what they want, and they want it immediately and will pursue their ambitions relentlessly. They hate delays, and can be impatient and intolerant. They have strong egos and need new challenges and constant flattery to be really happy. They hate to take advice and can be bossy, but will never bear grudges. Their generous and bawdy natures make them fun companions, but if they feel excitement is lacking, you can rely on them to generate a few crises to liven things up!

Perfect partner: Gemini.

Disasters: Cancer.

TAURUS *20 April – 20 May*

Gentle, affectionate and conservative, Taureans love their homes and families above all else. They are not terribly ambitious and their cautious natures thrive under routine. They can be snobbish and are great social climbers but are poor judges of character. They are masters of self-restraint, but underlying that placid facade is an extremely sensuous nature that often finds release in a tendency for laziness and a love of good food. Relationships are a priority for Taureans, and they fall in love easily and passionately. If love goes wrong, they will often persevere and remain in loveless marriages.

Perfect partner: Cancer.

Disasters: Scorpio.

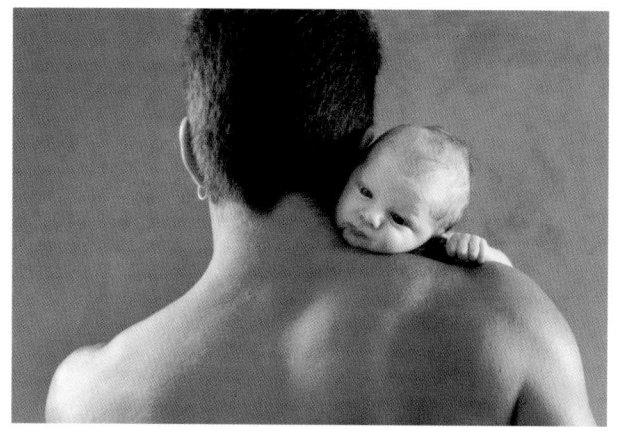

The greatest gift is a portion of thyself.

Ralph Waldo Emerson (1803–1882)

STAR SIGNS

GEMINI *21 May – 20 June*

The proverbial split personality, Geminis treasure clarity and reason. Often highly strung, Geminis are always overloaded with countless projects, none of which they explore in any depth. Their ready wit and lively minds make them popular, but often they are lacking in the long-term commitment that's necessary to make lasting friendships. Don't expect them to keep a secret – they love gossip and are always ready for a discussion as long as it's not about their emotions. They can be moody and emotionally immature. They need some freedom to be happily married, and partners should be prepared for them to indulge in a few dalliances.

Perfect partner: Libra.

Disasters: Virgo.

CANCER *21 June – 22 July*

Caring, considerate and committed, Cancerians seem made for the institution of marriage. They love their homes and are often great hoarders. Underneath their tough shells they are highly sensitive emotionally, and can easily feel rejected. They grow stronger when faced with adversity. They are often very sensual, but they try to hide their feelings from all but a privileged few. They are tenacious, and can be calculating. Don't expect them to spill the beans the first time you meet them – they'll hold themselves in check till they're sure you're worth the commitment, then attach themselves to you with Superglue! They are incredibly loyal and loving partners, even when the going gets tough.

Perfect partners: Taurus, Leo.

Disasters: Sagittarius, Aquarius.

STAR SIGNS

LEO *23 July – 22 August*

Warm, creative and generous, Leos demand the lion's share of attention. They crave constant approval and have a strong urge for self-expression – many end up in the theatre and those who don't still act as if they are stars. They need to achieve their goals to be happy, and if thwarted or angered can be deadly. Some Leos are overconfident and vain, but equally many are truly charismatic. Leos are moody and veer to extremes. If they don't acquire some self-knowledge they can be strident egotists. They plunge into love affairs, and usually have plenty of admirers if they learn not to be too overbearing.

Perfect partners: Gemini, Cancer.

Disasters: Capricorn.

VIRGO *23 August – 22 September*

Thoughtful, meticulous and critical, Virgos seem to have invented the word perfectionist. With their eye for detail and conscientious natures, they will accept only the highest of standards in everything. Because of this they have a tendency to be workaholics and are motivated by a strong sense of duty. They love gossip and their sharp wit can be malicious. Because of their tendency to rationalise, they often find relationships difficult, and will analyse everything to the utmost extreme. They usually marry late, and often never walk down the aisle, but once committed make dependable, caring and considerate companions.

Perfect partners: Cancer, Taurus.

Disasters: Sagittarius.

STAR SIGNS

LIBRA *23 September – 22 October*

Charming, graceful, fair-minded Librans often top the popularity polls, and they make a special effort to present a smiling face to the world. They are diplomatic, and will go out of their way to avoid arguments in their constant search for harmony in all things. This can make them seem a little bland or two-faced at times, but they are only trying to please everyone all the time. They suppress anger, and this often leads to stress-related illnesses. They love things of beauty and will make an extra effort to get the means to afford an elegant lifestyle. Having a partner is essential for Librans, and although they are very accommodating they like to feel they are in control emotionally.
Perfect partners: Librans will make a success of any relationship but Sagittarius is an especially good combination.

SCORPIO *23 October – 21 November*

Strong, resourceful Scorpios are personalities of extremes. They are able to endure physical and emotional hardships and their behaviour can fluctuate from spiritual to debauched. Their intense natures thrive on crises, which give them the opportunity to let off steam, and they are often their own worst enemies. They make devoted and committed friends but, if they sense betrayal, beware – they make relentless foes. They can be moody, but thrive in a loving, secure environment. They are known for their strong sexual energy but cherish a relationship that is equally as stimulating mentally and spiritually.
Perfect partners: Cancer, Libra.
Disasters: Aries, Gemini, Scorpio.

STAR SIGNS

SAGITTARIUS *22 November – 21 December*

Friendly, open, generous and vibrant, Sagittarians can be guaranteed to liven up any occasion. If they offend you with their frank remarks, remember that they are rarely malicious, and that they suffer from speak-first-and-think-later syndrome. They are always travelling in a bid to ease those ever-itchy feet. They love to mix with the "in" crowd and can be rather snobbish. They hate any restraint on their ebullient spirits and though they'll run through lovers at a rate of knots, they'll be very reticent about tying themselves to any one person.

Perfect partners: Virgo, Libra.

Disasters: Cancer, Scorpio.

CAPRICORN *22 December – 19 January*

Determined, practical and reliable, Capricorns will reach the positions of power and authority they crave no matter what. Their ambitions can lead them to be opportunistic and domineering, but underneath their stern facades they are often just great big softies. Although they seem reserved, if they're surrounded by friends you could be surprised by how decadent and outgoing they are. They are natural leaders and hate being subservient, though given power they can be tyrannical. They are artistic and frequently become involved in some sort of spiritual quest. They make loyal, faithful companions, although they're often a little emotionally insensitive.

Perfect partners: Virgo, Taurus.

Disasters: Gemini.

ANNIVERSARIES

1st	Paper	13th	Lace
2nd	Cotton	14th	Ivory
3rd	Leather	15th	Crystal
4th	Silk or flowers	20th	China
5th	Wood	25th	Silver
6th	Iron or candy	30th	Pearl
7th	Copper or wool	35th	Coral
8th	Bronze or rubber	40th	Ruby
9th	Pottery	45th	Sapphire
10th	Tin	50th	Gold
11th	Steel	55th	Emerald
12th	Linen	60th	Diamond

What's in a name?
That which we call a rose
By any other name would smell as sweet.

William Shakespeare (1564–1616)

BIRTHSTONES

January	Garnet – Constancy and truth
February	Amethyst – Sincerity and humility
March	Aquamarine – Courage and energy
April	Diamond – Innocence and success
May	Emerald – Tranquillity
June	Pearl – Preciousness and purity
July	Ruby – Freedom from care and chastity
August	Moonstone – Joy
September	Sapphire – Hope and chastity
October	Opal – Reflective of every mood
November	Topaz – Fidelity and loyalty
December	Turquoise – Love and success

FLOWERS

January	Snowdrop – Pure and gentle
February	Carnation – Bold and brave
March	Violet – Modest
April	Lily – Virtuous
May	Hawthorn – Bright and hopeful
June	Rose – Beautiful
July	Daisy – Wide-eyed and innocent
August	Poppy – Peaceful
September	Morning Glory – Easily contented
October	Cosmos – Ambitious
November	Chrysanthemum – Cheeky and cheerful
December	Holly – Full of foresight

Gift List

Name _____ Date _____

Gift _____

Name _____ Date _____

Gift _____

Name _____ Date _____

Gift _____

Name _____ Date _____

Gift _____

Name _____ Date _____

Gift _____

Name _____ Date _____

Gift _____

Name _____ Date _____

Gift _____

Gift List

Name _____ Date _____

Gift _____

Name _____ Date _____

Gift _____

Name _____ Date _____

Gift _____

Name _____ Date _____

Gift _____

Name _____ Date _____

Gift _____

Name _____ Date _____

Gift _____

Name _____ Date _____

Gift _____

Christmas List

Name	Year

Gift

Name	Year

Gift

Name	Year

Gift

Name	Year

Gift

Name	Year

Gift

Name	Year

Gift

Name	Year

Gift

Christmas List

Name _____ Year _____
Gift _____

Name _____ Year _____
Gift _____

Name _____ Year _____
Gift _____

Name _____ Year _____
Gift _____

Name _____ Year _____
Gift _____

Name _____ Year _____
Gift _____

Name _____ Year _____
Gift _____